What's
For
Dinner?

copyright

Dedicated to my mother

A first-class magician
in the kitchen.

foreword

This book offers our children, extended family, and beloved community food for the soul. I was fortunate to taste Donald's cooking soon after we met. He let me know that my cheese, olives, and fig spread (charcuterie trays) were not going to work for him. With his suave, easy-going style he also let me know without saying a word that he would be doing the cooking and, surprisingly, I never said a word.

At the time, I was living in Aventura, Florida and he would drive south on Fridays after work into crazy Miami traffic. The Golden Girls, what we called my mom and her gambling posse at the time - my Tia Olga, and family friend, Tia Miralles, would join us before we dropped them off at their favorite casino.

For a family that believes that cooking is an outpouring of love and care, I can say that Donald captured my heart (and the hearts of the three golden girls after the first bite).

I recall one weekend he arrived on a Saturday for lunch (instead of the usual Friday evening for dinner) and on this particular afternoon he had cooked his now famous, and my favorite, oxtails. My mom, with all the drama and jubilant energy she exhibited when she tasted something yummy, seriously announced to her audience that from that moment forward Donald's place was the head of the table. It worried me, if this is what she offered after an oxtail dish what would be her ask as she continued trying the collection of his favorite dishes specially those curated for this book with so much love and care?

I was raised in a family where the act of cooking was a wordless expression of "happy to see you, now allow me to take care of you and make everything better." This evokes vivid memories of me arriving home in the late hours after an exhausting work trip and seeing that my mother had stayed up to greet me with a pot of chicken soup on the stove ready to serve. Today, Donald honors that ritual in my mother's name but instead of the chicken soup at the end of a trip, or a long week, he makes the beef soup. And while chicken and beef soups are very different, in the language of cooking and love they mean the same.

Thank you, Donald, for pouring your heart and love into each of these perfectly prepared and measured recipes. Thank you for feeding our souls.

- *Mercedes Martin* -

introduction

It took a long time for me to accept something that friends and family had been telling me for decades... I know how to cook. Ok, I'm being modest. It has been said that I am an excellent cook. I have my doubts and, after preparing a meal, I'm always asking myself "now how can I make that taste better?"

There have been times, however, when I taste something that I have prepared and instead of a question, I end up saying... "Wow! That is good!" The problem is, I am not able to replicate that exact meal because I don't take note of the precise recipe and method. I am always experimenting. Always trying to discover how different blends of ingredients, temperature and time affect the final outcome.

When I decided to write this book, I realized that my biggest challenge was going to be the "how" in my creations. Several years ago, when I started teaching my son how to cook, I remember telling him that I do not know how to measure ingredients. The "how" was something that came from the heart. You figured out how much salt, black pepper, onions, garlic, etc. to add to that protein not by some written instruction but by how you felt inside. You literally have to develop a connection with that beef, pork or chicken and that will help you decide when to stop. Of course, a little experience helps as well. This is probably easier to do if you already enjoy cooking. Cooking is an adventure and, if you approach it as if it is a chore, that adventure can easily turn into a nightmare.

So, when I said earlier that my biggest problem would be the how, it was a reference to the fact that I would not be able to just sit and write down a bunch of recipes. I would have to cook each item three or more times so that I could determine (as best as possible) what precise measurements should be used for each ingredient.

As you try each recipe, you will notice that I specify brand names for some of the ingredients. This is not out of some sense of loyalty toward any brand. It is based purely on the fact that, after trying different brands over many years, these are the ones that work best for me.

As far as ingredients go, the pimento is one of my secret weapons. It is full of flavor and can easily overpower everything else in your pot. So please use with caution. And try to remember not to bite into these berries. They are not pleasing to the pallet.

There was a period in 2014 when I started cooking profusely because a leg injury kept me from going out to run, and I had nothing else to do. All my cooking at that time was on stove top and I realized that a pressure cooker would allow me to move faster and do more. My research led me to purchase my first multi cooker. You will find that most of the recipes in the following pages call for the use of this time-saving device. If you do not have one, then cook that protein for an additional hour (or more) until tender. Or stir that rice and peas until it reaches the desired consistency. Or get yourself a multi cooker. It will save you so much time in the kitchen.

Welcome to my adventure. If you follow along carefully, you will enjoy the ride.

table of contents

beef short ribs

It would be natural to start at the beginning but that's not happening here. I had never tried my hand at short ribs until maybe 2017, so my experience with this protein is relatively new. However, I think I have done enough to present you with something respectable.

This irresistible cut of beef is just bursting with flavor and tenderness. Short ribs done right is extremely delicious but be careful, it has a very high fat content.

ingredients

2 lbs. beef short ribs (4 or 5 pieces)
1 tsp. salt
½ tsp. finely ground pepper
2 tsp. Grace All Purpose Seasoning
4 cloves garlic (chopped)
3 slices medium-sized onion
6 to 10 whole pimento berries
1 tbsp. soy sauce
⅓ tsp. Badia Crushed Red Pepper (optional)
½ tsp. Badia Italian Seasoning

method

Add all ingredients except the Italian Seasoning, red pepper, and soy sauce to the meat and rub vigorously. Allow to marinate overnight or at least for a few hours.
Place the ribs in a hot pressure cooker. Add ½ cup of water after three minutes and cook for 80 minutes.
Add the remaining ingredients and continue cooking over low heat on stove top for another 20 to 30 minutes.
Skim or carefully pour off the oil from the surface of your gravy.
Serves 2 or 3.

oxtail

The tail of the ox was once considered unfit for human consumption. Now it's a delicacy and favorite to many. The recipe that I grew up with, called for the addition of butter beans towards the end of the cooking process. One day, I realized that I had run out of butter beans and, rather than going to the store, I quickly decided to try something else. Miniature dumplings. It was a hit. Not long after, I tried carrots and that worked well, too. Now when I cook this dish, I use one or the other, or both.

ingredients

2 lbs. Oxtail cut to maximum 1.25" thickness
1 tsp. salt
¼ tsp. finely ground black pepper
4 slices medium-sized onion
4 cloves garlic (chopped)
2 tsp. Grace All-Purpose Seasoning
⅓ tsp. Badia Crushed Red Pepper (optional)
5 - 8 whole pimento berries
½ tsp. Badia Italian Seasoning
2 tbsp. soy sauce
1 tsp. Grace Fish and Meat Sauce or Gray's Spicy Sauce
Optional items: flour (for mini dumplings), butter beans, carrots.

method

Cut away any excess fat and boil the oxtail for about 5 minutes. This helps to remove impurities, some of the embedded fat, and also prevents an aftertaste. Season with the salt, black pepper, onions, garlic, pimento, All Purpose Seasoning, and soy sauce. Allow to marinate overnight or at least for a few hours.

For up to two pounds of oxtail, cook under pressure for seventy (70) minutes. Add another ten (10) minutes per pound for up to four (4) pounds. If you want to prepare more than four (4) pounds of oxtail, consider using two pots. This will ensure a more even cook so that any one piece of meat will be just as tender the other.

Add the meat to the pressure cooker only after it gets hot. Wait for about three (3) minutes and add one half of a cup of water before covering.

When pressuring is complete, the meat is usually ready to be eaten. However, this is not always the case, and you should not hesitate to pressure for at least another thirty (30) minutes. Conduct a fork test and, when ready, complete cooking on stovetop.

Add the Italian Seasoning, crushed red pepper and Spicy Sauce.

It is not necessary to transfer all the liquid from the pressure cooker. You are making a gravy and should be able to do so over low heat within 20 to 30 minutes.

Options:
During that last 20 minutes, add a can of butter beans (drained) to your pot. Or, add ½ cup of chopped carrots. Or, add some miniature dumplings. Make these by adding a pinch of salt to 2 tbsp of flour. Add just enough water to knead the flour into a firm dough. Pinch and roll small pieces of the dough and add to your pot.

Any one of the above options will give you a tasty dish. Enjoy!

pumpkin beef soup

Of all the recipes in this book, this one will likely raise the ire of the Jamaican community more than any other. However, if you bear with me and give it a chance, you will agree that it does work.

ingredients

1.5 lb. beef shank (with bone)
1 lb. fresh pumpkin
1 whole choate (cho cho)
2 medium-sized carrots
3 tbsp. salt
¼ tsp. Badia Crushed Red Pepper (optional)
½ tsp. Badia Italian Seasoning
6 – 8 whole pimento berries
4 cloves garlic
1 packet Grace Pumpkin Soup

method

Cut the beef shank into small pieces and boil for about five minutes. This will remove impurities and reduce the oiliness of the meat. Pour off the hot water and rinse with cold. Set seven cups of water to boil in your pressure cooker. Trim the pumpkin and cut into chunks. Trim the choate, remove the heart and slice into strips. Cut the carrots into small pieces (discs or julienne).

Add the meat, pumpkin, choate, carrots, garlic, and pimento to the pressure cooker. Seal and set to cook for seventy (70) minutes.

Crush the chunks of pumpkin and add the salt, red pepper, Italian seasoning, and the packet of pumpkin soup as you transfer to stovetop to continue cooking.

Cook for another thirty minutes over low heat.

curried chicken

This is a relatively quick and tasty dish that goes well over a bed of white rice, with some fried ripe plantains served on the side. You will find that, apart from the curry powder, the garlic and pimento play a huge part in infusing flavor into this dish.

ingredients

Approximately 2 lbs. of chicken
(preferably the leg, thigh, and hips) chopped
1 tsp. salt
¼ tsp. finely ground black pepper
4 cloves of garlic (chopped)
6 – 8 whole pimento berries
¼ tsp. Badia Crushed Red Pepper (optional)
½ cup of chopped or julienned carrots
½ tsp. Badia Italian Seasoning
3 tbsp. Grace Curry Powder
1 tbsp. cooking oil

method

Remove any excess fat from the chicken pieces. Wash and drain the chicken. Add all the seasoning and let marinate overnight.

When your pot is hot, reduce heat to medium and add the cooking oil. Wait one minute then add the chicken. Leave uncovered for five minutes and stir at least twice, then cover the pot. The chicken will produce its own liquid within a minute. If this does not happen, add a quarter cup of water.

Adjust heat to low and cook for one hour, stirring every twenty minutes. Approximately ten minutes before completion, add carrots and stir for an even distribution. You can substitute the carrots with small, diced potatoes, or use both together. Before removing from heat, make sure that the liquid has reduced enough to form a nice, rich gravy.

baked chicken wings

Who doesn't like a serving of baked wings? They make great appetizers and, sometimes, they are satisfying enough to serve as the entrée. It took me a while to get these to a point where I felt satisfied with the end result. Now I am being told that these are "super tasty." (Thank you for that endorsement, Tres Mercedes!)

I like to use about nine wings for this recipe. This is because you will want each piece to have enough room during the first 40 minutes of the baking process to get that crispiness on the outside. That way, even after adding the sauce for the final 10 minutes, your chicken will still be a little crispy but with enough tenderness to be falling off the bone.

ingredients

9 chicken wings
Season the wings with:
1 tsp. salt
¼ tsp. finely ground black pepper
½ tsp. paprika
2 tsp. Grace All Purpose Seasoning

Sauce Mixture:
4 tbsp. soy sauce
1 tbsp. Grace Fish and Meat Sauce
½ cup orange juice
1 tbsp. honey
½ tbsp. Badia Italian Seasoning
¼ tsp. Crushed Red Pepper
Water (enough to bring mixture to 1 cup)

method

Bake at 420° for 20 minutes. Turn each piece and bake for another 20 minutes. Mix the sauce, pour over each piece of chicken and bake at 350° for 10 minutes. Remove from oven and let rest uncovered before serving.

pan seared sea bass

I will usually declare that I don't cook fish unless it's salted cod or pickled mackerel. However, here is a recipe I developed that has found favor with many.

ingredients

1.5 lbs. Chilean sea bass
(preferably with the skin on)
1 tsp. salt
¼ tsp. black pepper
1 tbsp. olive oil
3 slices (medium sized) onion
4 cloves garlic
1 tsp. Badia Italian Seasoning
1 tbsp. unsalted butter
½ tsp. Badia Crushed Red Pepper (optional)

method

Sprinkle fish with the salt and black pepper. Rub and spread lightly with fingers, or the back of a spoon. Put aside.

Using a large skillet, bring to medium heat. Add the olive oil, wait 30 seconds then add your fish, skin side down. Cook the fish for four minutes on each side. Two minutes before completion, add butter, onions, and garlic. Remove the fish from the skillet and reduce the heat to low. Be sure to place your fish skin side down. Add the Italian seasoning and pepper to the skillet. Let simmer for four minutes, stirring occasionally.

Pour sauce over fish, turn skin side up and serve with ½ lemon, (if desired).

curried goat

This is another dish utilizing curry, which is an undoubtedly fine ingredient that goes a long way towards elevating mutton. This recipe works just as well with lamb.

ingredients

Two lbs. of fresh goat meat, cut in ½-inch cubes. The cut does not have to be in cubes. Small pieces will do just as well.
1 tsp. Salt
½ tsp. Ground Black Pepper
4 cloves Garlic
6 to 8 Whole Pimento berries
¼ tsp. Badia Dried Red Pepper (optional)
½ tsp. Badia Italian seasoning
½ cup of diced potatoes (optional)
½ cup chopped carrots (optional)

method

Cut away any excess fat from the meat. Add all the seasoning, rub vigorously, and let marinate overnight.

Unlike the process for curried chicken, it is better to use a pressure cooker when preparing mutton. Otherwise, the process could take hours to reach the desired tenderness. Seventy (70) minutes should be adequate for two pounds of mutton. Add the meat to the pot only after the pot gets hot. Wait for about three (3) minutes then add a half cup of water, if necessary. Cover and secure.

When pressuring is complete, the meat is usually ready to be eaten. However, this is not always the case, and you should not hesitate to pressure for at least another thirty (30) minutes. Conduct a fork test and, when ready, complete cooking on stovetop.

It is not necessary to transfer all the liquid from the pressure cooker. Cook over low heat for another (twenty) 20 minutes. This will reduce the liquid to gravy. If you want to, go ahead and add some chopped carrots or potatoes, and sprinkle some more Italian seasoning for an additional burst of flavor. Stir to distribute evenly. Before removing from heat, make sure that the liquid has reduced enough to form a nice, rich gravy.

rack of lamb

It's been less than a year since I decided (with great encouragement) to move up from preparing lamb shoulder (an excellent curried dish) to preparing rack of lamb. I must admit that I like the outcome even though lamb was not one of my favorites.

ingredients

1 Frenched (rib bones exposed) lamb rack with 7 to 8 ribs (1½ to 2 lbs.)
2 tbsp. Badia Italian Seasoning
¼ tsp. Badia Crushed Red Pepper (optional)
2 cloves garlic, minced
2 slices onion, minced
1 tsp. salt
¼ tsp. ground black pepper
2 tbsp. extra virgin olive oil

method

Add one tablespoon of olive oil to a hot skillet and sear both sides of the lamb.

Preheat the oven to 400° and mix (preferably with a food processor) the remaining ingredients into a paste. Score the fat, sprinkle lightly with additional salt and pepper (if desired), spread the paste onto the fat side, wrap the exposed bones in foil, and place in roasting pan fat side up. Roast for 25 minutes.

Remove from oven, cover with foil, and let rest for 15 minutes. Serves 3 to 4.

pork chops

This is a personal favorite, and a challenge as well. As with chicken wings, I had to experiment with different methods before coming up with a satisfactory recipe.

ingredients

2 pork chops, preferably 1½ inch thick
1 tsp. salt
¼ tsp. finely ground black pepper
4 cloves garlic (chopped)
2 to 3 slices medium sized onion
1 tsp. Grace All Purpose Seasoning
½ tsp. Badia Italian Seasoning
¼ tsp. Badia Crushed Red Pepper (optional)
2 tbsp. soy sauce
1 tsp. Gray's Spicy Sauce or Grace Fish and Meat Sauce
2 tbsp. brown sugar
1 tbsp. extra virgin olive oil

method

Sprinkle both sides of your pork chops with the salt, black pepper and All Purpose seasoning. Use your fingers or the back of a spoon to spread evenly and rub into the meat.

Add olive oil to a hot large skillet. Bring temperature to medium and add the pork chops, searing both sides for about five minutes or until golden brown. Remove from skillet and set aside.

Add the remaining ingredients to a measuring cup with enough water to bring the total mixture to ¾ cup. Stir vigorously to dissolve the sugar.

Set your oven to 350 degrees. Place your pork chops in an oven safe container, pour the mixture evenly over both pieces seal tightly and bake for twenty (20) minutes. If your chops are less than 1½ inches thick, bake for fifteen (15) minutes instead of twenty. Enjoy with your choice of sides.

rice and peas

I am not sure about the history of what we Jamaicans fondly refer to as rice and peas. I grew up having this served as part of that special Sunday dinner that my mother or grandmother would make.

Rice and peas is actually made with red kidney beans, which is substituted with pigeon peas (gungu peas) on special occasions. One of the things that I enjoy about cooking rice and peas is the fact that your nose can help with the process. As you move from stage two to three and from three to four, you can detect a change in the aroma, as the flavors come together. That change is an indication of when to move forward.

Once again, I am reminding the traditionalists, the purists, and the experts to keep in mind that all the recipes in this book reflect methods that I have developed over several years.

ingredients

2.5 cups white rice
¾ cup red kidney beans
1 cup coconut milk
7 cups water
3 tbsp. salt
1 tsp. Badia Italian Seasoning
^{1}/3 tsp. Badia Crushed Red Pepper (optional)

method

Boil the beans until tender (cook under pressure for 60 to 70 minutes.) Add the pepper and Italian seasoning and continue cooking at medium, low heat. When the aroma changes (or after 6 to 8 minutes), add the coconut milk. Let the mixture continue cooking and turn off your heat source after another 6 to 8 minutes (or when the aroma changes). Wash and add the rice. Add the salt and stir for an even distribution of all the ingredients. Cook until the rice achieves the desired consistency. To eliminate guesswork, I use the rice cooker setting of my multi cooker for this step.

Serve with your favorite protein.

potato salad

Even those of us who believe that potatoes should be avoided will admit that it's not such a bad thing to veer off course occasionally. It's even better when we veer off course for a tasty potato salad.

ingredients

3 large Russet potatoes
1 boiled egg (finely chopped)
1 onion slice (chopped)
½ can Mixed Vegetables
(Del Monte preferred)
¼ tsp. paprika
$1/8$ tsp. finely ground black pepper
1 tsp. Badia Italian Seasoning
$1/8$ tsp. Badia Crushed Red Peppers
(optional)
6 tbsp. mayonnaise

method

Set 6 cups of water to boil. Peel and dice the potatoes and add to the boiling water. Boil for 15 minutes and drain.

Add the remaining ingredients and mix to make sure that everything is spread evenly.

This salad can be served with any of the proteins described earlier in this book.

Happy eating!

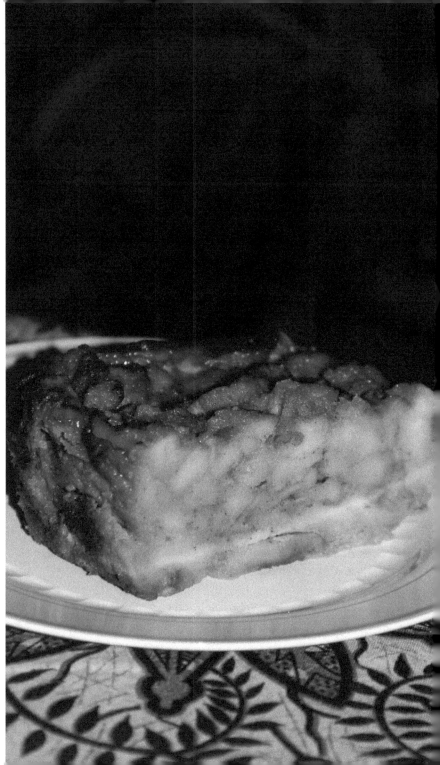

bread pudding

I decided to revive this old favorite after many disappointments at restaurants where the bread pudding was the highly recommended dessert. This item does not need to be complicated and should not be dry when served. A good bread pudding should not need to have a sauce added to delight the palate.

After a more than thirty-years hiatus, I decided to get back to making my own bread pudding. Here is a very simple but effective recipe.

ingredients

4 cups bread cubes (about 4 slices of your favorite bread, toasted and cut or torn into cubes)
2 ¼ cups milk (whole milk, please; lactose free, if necessary)
2 eggs, beaten
¾ cup brown sugar
¼ cup raisins (optional)
½ tsp. ground cinnamon
1 tsp. vanilla extract
1 tsp. rum extract
¼ tsp. salt

method

Soak the bread cubes in the milk for a few hours (preferably overnight). Stir in the remaining ingredients, pour into a 9-inch greased baking dish or standard bread loaf pan. Bake at 350° for 45 minutes or until your knife comes out clean.

Super simple and very tasty.

Lightning Source UK Ltd.
Milton Keynes UK
UKHW022104130223
416963UK00015B/215